THE COLOURS OF THE FOREST

OTHER BOOKS BY TOM WAYMAN

Poetry

Waiting For Wayman, 1973
For and Against the Moon: Blues, Yells, and Chuckles, 1974
Money and Rain: Tom Wayman Live!, 1975
Free Time: Industrial Poems, 1977
A Planet Mostly Sea, 1979
Living on the Ground: Tom Wayman Country, 1980
Introducing Tom Wayman, 1980
The Nobel Prize Acceptance Speech, 1981
Counting the Hours: City Poems, 1983
The Face of Jack Munro, 1986
In a Small House on the Outskirts of Heaven, 1989
Did I Miss Anything?, 1993
The Astonishing Weight of the Dead, 1994
I'll Be Right Back, 1997

Essays

Inside Job: Essays on the New Work Writing, 1983
A Country Not Considered: Canada, Culture, Work, 1993

Editor

Beaton Abbot's Got the Contract, 1974
A Government Job at Last, 1976
Going for Coffee, 1981
East of Main (with Calvin Wharton), 1989
Paperwork, 1991

The Colours of the Forest

poems by

Tom Wayman

HARBOUR PUBLISHING

Harbour Publishing
P.O. Box 219
Madeira Park, BC V0N 2H0 Canada

Harbour Publishing acknowledges the financial support of the
Government of Canada through the Book Publishing Industry
Development Program (BPIDP) and the Canada Council for the
Arts, and the Province of British Columbia through the British
Columbia Arts Council for its publishing activities.

Cover design and illustration by Roger Handling
Printed and bound in Canada

Canadian Cataloguing in Publication Data

Wayman, Tom, 1945–
    The colours of the forest

    Poems.
    ISBN 1-55017-202-6

    I. Title.
PS8595.A9C64 1999   C811'.54   C99-910190-0
PR9199.3.W39C64 1999

THE CANADA COUNCIL | LE CONSEIL DES ARTS
FOR THE ARTS | DU CANADA
SINCE 1957 | DEPUIS 1957

ACKNOWLEDGEMENTS

I am grateful for the support for my work shown by the editors of the following publications in which poems here first were published: *Arc, Caliban, The Canadian Forum, Canadian Literature, Denver Quarterly, Event, The Fiddlehead, The Malahat Review, The New Quarterly, The Ohio Review, Ontario Review, Passages North, Poetry Northwest, Prairie Fire, Quarry, Queen's Quarterly, Split Shift* (Los Angeles). "The Colours of the Forest" appeared first in *The Hudson Review;* "Excavation" was first printed in *The Iowa Review;* "The Nest," "Poetry Overdose" and "When We Parted" were first published in *TriQuarterly,* a publication of Northwestern University.

"Billy's Peccadillos" and "The Turn of the Tide" were anthologized in *Getting By* (Bottom Dog Press, 1996). "Poetry Overdose" and "Billy On Industrial Progress" were included in my *Did I Miss Anything? Selected Poems 1973–1993* from Harbour Publishing (1993). "The Alts Visit," "Autumn's Gate," "The Bald Man," "The Big O," "The Burial of the Clown," "The Call," "The Death of the Clown," "For William Stafford," "The Hallows," "I'll Be Right Back," "In a House of Women," "Insertion," "The Monument to the Clown," "Post-Secondary Education," "The Quarrel," "The Road's Side," and "Where Mountain Water" were included in my *I'll Be Right Back: New and Selected Poems 1980–1996* from Ontario Review Press (1997). Many thanks to Howard White of Harbour Publishing and Raymond J. Smith of Ontario Review Press for permission to reprint these poems here.

The creation of this book was also greatly assisted by grants from The Canada Council for the Arts and from the Project Assistance for Creative Writers program of the B.C. Arts Council. I very much appreciate the writing time provided me by these awards.

Contents

Autumn's Gate

THE HALLOWS

A road in the moonlight
and the roses are trembling

What passes down the lane
crosses the dark shadows of trees

toward a house, where leaves are piled on soil
in which tulip bulbs are buried

amid ground-up bones
soaked with water

which will be preserved as liquid
in the frozen earth all winter

What touches the road
is neither wheel nor foot

nor hoof
nor the moon

nor the roses by the gate
trembling

AUTUMN'S GATE

By afternoon, the road
began to enter an autumn country.
Ferns along the shoulder
blurred into brown
as yellow birch leaves
stirred
or floated
above the asphalt.

And I saw in a smoke or mist
that drifted on the hills
the doorway
through which eons of green Aprils,
white Decembers
have passed.

So much has crossed over
what is left to comfort
we who still gather
about autumn's gate?
I believe death may be more filled with
a joyful music
than this side retains.
I think of Blake greeting his death
with happy tunes
—what did he comprehend
of where he was to travel?

In nature's house are many mansions
a wise man said.
If death does not sweep us utterly away
what light streams
from those dwellings?

Are the dead like us who remain
—swung with the planet's turning
into a customary, complicated dark?
Or are the dead a faded smoke
from autumn's fires?

The highway climbs through a mottled wood
of orange larch and green fir.
I do not know if the dead
are lost
or found

or are themselves a road across these valleys
and ridges,
this season.

THE ALTS VISIT

They entered my head
as if they walked into another room of
their apartment
by the East River.
They brought their habitual
low-key bickering:
"We want to inform you, concerning Sara,"
Herschel said, "just so you know,
so you understand . . . "
"Herschel, we agreed
I'm to tell him," Edith cut Herschel off:
"Whenever your mother, whenever Sara
crosses over, we'll meet her.
She won't be alone.
Herschel and I . . . "
"We'll be there," Herschel interrupted,
"She'll be all right
with us." And then the speech mannerism
that helped define him while he was alive:
"Do you get the, uh . . . ? Do you get the, uh . . . ?"
"Herschel," Edith protested,
"let me finish:
someone is always present
to help when you cross," Edith said.
"Unless," she added, looking
above her half-glasses,
"a person feels he needs to
do this alone, experience this
by himself."
In the sudden silence, I knew Edith spoke
to the tension between
my fears of death and my fears of being
obligated to others.
"But we will meet Sara," Edith continued after a moment.
"Yes, we will," Herschel echoed
out of the dark.

TO WAIT WITH A PERSON DYING

All hours have collapsed
into this room, its air
dense with close-
packed molecules of
time

The borders of each moment
are charred, ragged
The black portions
slowly
    expand
transforming these minutes to
brittle flakes

In a corner
a figure clothed by shadow
reveals a face
white as a moon's
  —bone skin calcified
and pitted, from which radiates
a flickering gleam:
the expression in its eyes
neither merciless nor
compassionate
toward the bed

where a person's aged hands
pluck at
a sheet over her chest
pull up, then allow the cloth to settle
and again tug
    to lift
  release

THE HOUR OF OUR DEATH

Neither the minute
nor the absolute
instant is
referred to, but

at seven in the morning
a woman working nights at home care
emerges from the darkened bedroom
to greet her relief, who hangs her coat
in the hall closet, changes into indoor shoes
from boots stained with the the March snowmelt
and gravel
She had a restless night
the brief report of the darkness
is presented casually, like gossip
She took some water on a sponge
when I last changed the sheets about four a.m.
She's dozing now
The newcomer walks into the sickroom
and approaches an elderly woman
lying on her back
alone in the double bed
The aged face is shut, except breath
enters and leaves in ragged bursts
but steadily
The woman on duty decides not to announce herself
until the patient wakes
She settles onto a chair to scan
the topmost of the stack of ruled paper
on which is recorded the significant events in this room
At eleven minutes past seven
the caregiver's eyes
sweep along handwriting
illuminated by a dim light
—a human brain
processes a series of scrawled lines
into an imagined yesterday, while the personality
that brain creates
considers simultaneously the next eight hours

At this moment, however, a world stops
A shift will end early

MY MOTHER'S BURIAL

Her own brain
struck at her left side
repeatedly
until she could not walk
    speak
  swallow
Who she was
boiled away
to a
breath
    kept in
            forever
    released

in-
    haled

Then a black van
brought two men
with a stretcher
onto which the husk
was tied
She was wheeled
down apartment
corridors
through sunlight
and loaded into
the cargo space

My father and brother
and I
followed that van
amid traffic
to the freeway
and an exit
beyond suburbs

where we parked on the shoulder of

a two-lane
highway
A wagon drawn by a pair of horses
waited
Two men climbed down
and unloaded an oblong box
from the back of
their wagon
and carried it to
the van
All four of
these servants of death
busied themselves
inside the rear of the van
When they emerged
my mother was
within the container of
auburn polished wood
that was hoisted once more
into the wagon
whose horses were urged
to pull
A short distance ahead
they turned north down a dirt road
Meantime a small crowd
had arrived by car
and all of us began to follow
on foot
the slowly-rotating wheels
of the wooden hearse
As we paced along
we dodged puddles
left by the early Spring rains
Steady thump
of the horses'
hooves
squeaks
from the wagon's
axles and frame
rustle of
the motion of clothing and boots

of the thirty or so of us
who walked

After some minutes
I noticed another open wagon
with a single horse
harnessed in its shafts
at a sideroad between
already-furrowed fields
This vehicle held
several people dressed like
Hutterites
or men and women in early photos
of eastern Europe
Their faces
shimmered
Each became more distinct
when we approached
but as their wagon lurched forward
to trail our clump of travellers
their features again
wavered
when I stared back at them

The road now curved amid
low wooded hills
and gullies through which
creeks wound
At one turn, as we trudged
I saw the route we followed
descend to the shore
of a huge lake
or sea
When we reached the water
and the wagon stopped
the morning had become hazy
A cool mist
had risen over the small inlet
or bay
Most of us sat or sprawled to rest
around the hearse

although the second band of mourners
did not step down
from their conveyance
About me I heard the low murmur
of conversation
the slap of leather reins
and a metallic rattle or chime
as horses tossed their heads
or shifted their feet
Waves
lapped successively
at pebbles and sand

The swirling mist
started to envelop us
Its chill breath
touched my hands and face
I could scarcely see
my brother hunkered down like a stone
between me and the wagon
Sudden cries
from near the water
Then I could distinguish people
scrambling upright
where the wooden prow of a boat
touched shore

A cluster of shadows
were unloading the coffin
and I could not be sure in the thick fog
if these were men and women I recognized
or were from
the second wagon
I stepped closer
but already those who lifted
my mother
were passing down the vehicle's other side
I hurried after
and watched them hoist the oblong box
onto the forward deck
where other hands and arms

carried the coffin aft
into mist
I saw shape after shape
wade a short distance
alongside the vessel
then scramble up
or be pulled on board
as the bow
began to slip
backwards
into the impenetrable white
At the edge of the water
my father, brother and I
witnessed a dim form
dissolve
and vanish

Behind us
only one wagon
was plodding up
the sunlit road, a single group
of mourners straggling after
A tangle of footprints remained
in the wet sand
of the beach
No other sign
marked this visitation here
this payment in full for a gift
this return of what had been borne
to its beginning

THE TURN OF THE TIDE

light flickers on the sere leaf
as a dry wind
nudges the underside

       when the train brakes to a halt
       the watcher on board perceives
       his car start to roll backwards

       and then it does

the green wind
bears the details of moisture
warmth, pollen

     as a mind
     contains and offers
     a party in the landlord's basement
     during the 1950s at Kitimat, the names of grandnieces
     the lineup for mission food
     in Tucson once
     pouring cement for the south tower
     of the Granville Street Bridge
     a Portuguese curse memorized
     with the help of a co-worker
     whose name was, whose name was

       the closest edge of the sea-foam
       dampens, then soaks
       a grain of sand

       the next tumble of water
       slides up the beach
       just short of that dark grain

a gardener
scoops handful after handful

of rich loam
from the bag he holds

he paces forward
scattering the redolent composted soil

across the ground
the gardener digs into the sack

all forenoon
afternoon

until he bends further
to reach into the container

appears stooped, shuffles
in his rough palm

hard granules show amid the
moist peat moss and earth

each dip into the bag
now draws more

ash-grey
bone meal

until his hands cup
only what has been

burned and crushed
this substance falls

between shaking fingers
into air

        the child's crayon
        does not want to stay within the lines
        printed on a page

        she pushes the colour strongly
        across the paper
        and onto the tablecloth

her line sets out

each wave
breaks spectacularly on the beach

while at the centre of the lion-headed
surf
an undertow calls back the water

to ocean's core

past Dryden station
the boxcar
cools in the fall night
when the chill grips him
he opens his bag
and removes a newspaper
he takes one sheet
scrunches it into a ball
places it beside him
then he lights the wadded paper, the flames
explode
the eyes of the other two men
in the car
turn toward the blaze
he warms his hands
as this fuel stiffens to black
crumbles
a minute later
he draws out another sheet

hammering and screech of the wheels

the paper dying and flaring

heat and ice

I'LL BE RIGHT BACK

When the last of my chairs
is loaded on the truck
I'll be right back

The boxes of books
wholesaled away, my files
and trunk full of mementos from childhood
bagged for the trash
I'll be right back

The last poem of mine
finally excised in the anthology revision
I'll be right back

When no one alive
remembers there was a person with my name
I'll be right back

And I don't mean reincarnation
And I don't mean
soul
I don't mean
we're all part of the biosphere
Nor do I mean
random evolutionary chance

I mean I'll be
right back

The Two Countries

FOR WILLIAM STAFFORD (1914–1993)

Travelling in the dusk, I hit a deer
on the Monashee Highway west of the Needles ferry

A brown blur
passed above the hood

then the metallic gasp and
thud of two vehicles that collide

The truck drove on
all the dashboard gauges normal

while I steered to the shoulder
and braked, the motor idling

On either side, forested mountains
bore their silent February snows

I rounded the front of the truck
and stopped: it had been caved in

as though I had struck a post
—the bumper bent outwards

to a semicircle, grill smashed
piercing the radiator, coolant leaking down

in weak streams
One headlight shone ahead

but the other was wrenched 90 degrees
through shattered glass

I mounted again
and swung the engine's final minutes

across the asphalt and back

to see the deer

which lay facing east
dead

one eye aimed toward me
like a rifle

or a gold coin burnished to a flash
or the illumination device

of a vessel
from a different sun

THE QUARREL

They had been out
getting firewood.
She thought going as a family
would be good: the children
could have a day
outdoors with their Dad. He
wanted to go with Rob,
his friend, in Rob's pickup
like the two of them did
almost every year,
but after the quarrel
about how could he stack logs
in a goddamn station wagon
full of kids, and she pointed out
without getting mad
they could use the trailer
he hauled the skidoo in,
he finally agreed
it was An Okay Idea.
But now he's pissed off
because you have to watch
those two kids every goddamn minute
so everything takes five times as long,
but mostly because
the chain saw choked and died
and he couldn't restart it
after trying six hundred times
and so the trailer is only half full
which means he'll have to come back again
by himself, since Rob went last weekend
knowing he was going to go this Sunday
with the goddamn Family,
and because now this completely worthless
piece of useless shit
of a car isn't starting either
and here they are up the back of beyond
and didn't he say you just don't take kids
cutting firewood
that it's not like a visit to a

stupid waterslide or something?

And he's walking up the logging road
to cool off, thinking
there's something wrong
with this, I shouldn't
be married
to her
And she's sitting alone in the
front seat, reassuring the children
in back,
telling herself *there's something wrong with*
me,
why aren't I
happy? I know he isn't perfect
but we're married
and every other couple we know
may have their troubles but
the wives seem content

And by March
she will have been living in a one-bedroom
motel suite, with the kids,
three months
although she tells her friends
it isn't as bad
as it seems:
the children could stay in the same
school
and one of their classmates even lives
at the motel,
and sooner or later some place
will come up she can afford
and it's not like
this is forever

THE TWO COUNTRIES

Far from the urban
Two countrysides
Exist concurrently

One savours the green
And the
Silence

Accepts what the wooded ridge says
The taste of lilac
And rain

The touch of a road
Smoothed across gravel and soil
The scent

Of fir seedlings
The other country
Is a frenzy to clearcut

To culvert, to layer asphalt
It believes in the loud metallic
Throbbing

Of stacked lumber
The stench of bright yard lights
Metal splinters

Of chainsaw and backhoe
Junked cars
Affixed in meadows

Like trophy heads
Of mule deer
On the outside of a tire repair shop

These rearrangements
Make of the verdant
Republic

The slovenly
Back yard
Of city

Yet neither of these two regions
Is found whole in one
Mind

The lovers of the gorgets
Of hummingbirds
Remove the pines in whose honor

A distant peak conceals itself
Some who pray hourly
To chaste water and air

Complain as often in season
About the infrequency of the district's snowplows
And another neighbor is proud

Equally of his bees
And black logging truck
For me

To restore the unified vision
Of rural or wilderness
Solitude

I must stand under the curve
Of my skull
On a hill, perhaps once cleared

But now a dense growth of
Birch or alder
Freshly leaved

By April or May
The slope watched
From each direction by mountains

Only into this landscape
Can I set or replace immediately
Any green thing that

Takes years to establish
To become presence
In earth, in the country

That is in my time
Two countries

OTHER POWERS

A chainsaw's intrusive
me-me-me-me

cannot conceal under such bragging
a throb of fear: *maybe*
my species
does not really control

but during a pause
the heavy *crump*
of a high birch or alder
landing
I feel ground shake
Then that whine
One more century or almost
staggers

On the lake
the wind pushes ahead
of summer thunder
I keep the canoe
quartering the multiplying
whitecaps, aim
for a gravel beach ahead
Troughs below my right shoulder
deepen
until my leg is abruptly soaked
as the top of a wave
lurches on board
Water flows past my feet
The bow tosses frenziedly
for an instant, my paddle
heaves us forward

I am aware
how loud the breakers are, the hiss here
of the surges
Spray continually
strikes me

I abandon my goal
swing with the waves
toward rocks of the closest shore

Three ravens
hunch on the ground under a small alder
in whose branches
a robin has nested this spring
The black birds
peck at
a small unravelled bundle
of twigs and straw
A robin
perches nearby on a fence rail
while the huge black forms
inspect
their work

until they exchange calls
harsh as a saw
glide down into the meadow
and flap to the cottonwood by the road
The smaller bird waits a few minutes
then hops along the rail
and disappears into the alder leaves
that nod in the rising breeze

TEACHERS AT RISK

The eyes of some teachers of adolescents
collapse inwards: become sumps
into which drain
downpours of hurt.
Too many semesters
students that these instructors admire
blurt out hateful
pronouncements: how badly a disruption in class
was resolved Wednesday, how stupid and boring
a subject is that this teacher
attempts to remain passionate about
—geometric logic, dreams, metalwork. A favored boy
who in January wrote
a tender portrait of his grandfather
is caught shoplifting in March
for drug money; a shy girl
encouraged for detected hints of
comic wit, who began to sparkle
in drama—innovative at mimicry
—starts to skip, to spend the day at a mall
with a boy's insolent, intrusive hands.
They're just kids, the teachers' mouths
plead with their eyes.
But an algae of disappointment,
of rage at disparaged effort
scums across corneas.
The instructors' faces take on the perplexed aspect
of a parent's who admits defeat: *I love my daughter*
but I can't stand what she does.

The vision of such teachers
skitter over the week's routine: lesson plans,
attendance, cafeteria monitor, and an appointment with
both sides of a divorce, reunited for a half-hour
in hostility toward this school's failure
to motivate their child. Eyes
recede into skulls
as if backing away from
a student who shrieks

at them, a father suddenly yelling threats,
a principal who cautions
not to take the job personally, not to care
so much. The eyes
are a bruise
these teachers deny
as a battered woman might: they attempt to ignore
the black agony that flows each hour
into the aqueous humor, cling rather to
any hallway or classroom
word or occurrence that supplies
even a brief
infusion of joy.

POST-SECONDARY EDUCATION

The moon appeared in the dark lake
the moment it crested the hills.

In my car speeding north, the student
I had given a lift to

said: "The old guys
should get out of our way." He meant

musicians, writers, politicians
—our conversation had shifted to the roots

of the present. "The aged need to step aside,
make room for the young."

The highway was four lanes
but not much traffic so late. The moon

had climbed above the eastern ridge now.
I didn't say

Perhaps the people you mention
waited years

to achieve their status.
What if they intend to savour

where they are? Should they disappear
because you're as impatient

as they were once?
And I didn't say

Look at the full moon
racing us up the lake.

I didn't say
How beautiful the moon is

high over the valley rim.
I held onto the wheel

and I drove.

THE FERRYMAN

Step into my craft
and I will try to carry you over.

When we cast off, and I begin to pole
the vessel toward the further shore,

I will ask your aid,
willing, or half-willing,

that is my fee—a lookout ahead for rocks
and upstream for logs,

extra hands set to oars,
or pumps below if needed—

until the landing place approaches
beside trees rising from jumbled stones,

and you can disembark
again.

At times I tire of the life
—heaving this boat from dock to dock

season after season,
the passengers nervous or indifferent.

When I began I was not the ferryman
but just myself, hired to stand at the stern

on a bright autumn morning, a fog
covering the river

until the sun cleared the mountain.
Crossing by crossing, though,

I grew into the role
and then I answered easily to the name:

Ferryman
although, like everyone, I am always more than

a category, or employee.
In this work on the water

I take pleasure in the excitement of most of you
as we near the other bank:

a glad anticipation of unloading,
a collection of yourselves, your belongings,

attachments. A few on board express gratitude
and I remind them

we have traversed a river, not a sea,
that no matter which shore we have reached

the road ahead still points to that larger voyage.
Yet I envy you occasionally,

your journeying. Though each trip here
is unique, I confess I feel a dulling

of my responses to what I encounter:
no longer awed, for instance,

by the white cottonwood tufts
buoyed, lifting or descending,

on the currents above the July flow.
And I worry that my task

will mean I never view again
wonders beyond this valley.

My solace is to focus on time
and texture: the pilgrim who tells me

I carried her mother once,
or another that reports she took this trip with me

a decade ago;
the heft of rope, paddle,

of the pole easy in my hand,
or my calmness during a night crossing

in Spring flood: the loud river that tosses spray
over the gunwale, soaking the travellers

huddled on thwarts under canvas,
and that threatens the lanterns guttering

on the deck. Though my course may be dangerous
I am confident I can bring

my cargo safely to land.
I dream my years of

conveying you
are a row of holes I dibble

in a garden's soil,
where I place

seed after seed after seed
in the Earth's open mouths.

SORRY MY PAPER IS LATE, BUT

We had a power failure and I couldn't use my computer
My spell-check broke
You're never in your office
so I couldn't speak to you about a topic

I was away when you announced the assignment
and nobody told me about it
The material you asked us to read was too long
All the books in the library were out

My mother made me take our dog to the vet
There was a movie on TV I really, really wanted to watch
I gave the essay to my sister's boyfriend to hand in for me
and he drove to Vancouver and it's still in his car
I don't understand why we need to do this paper

I have a life, you know

SEMESTER'S END

The point of my pen sways, then
touches down inside a square ruled on paper
to imprint a mark, a grade.
A column of these squares, each containing a letter,
resembles a strand of barbed wire
whose evenly-spaced twists with honed ends
threaten or inflict sufficient pain
to bring certain motions to a stop.

What do the chisel-edges of the barbs
aim to confine or exclude?
These projections surely have their origin
in the knots tied in the cords of a lash
or knout—the punisher
of those whose actions refute the will
of the wielder, or of those who order
this agony imposed.

I will not speak of the men and women
my pen has beaten into silence,
into a surly abasement or dejection.

For a few, the stultifying alphabet of pain
when applied to their skin
is interpreted as praise.
Their sincere efforts, their service
are rewarded by my pen with a letter
they have been convinced to regard as an honor.
But the ink figure
discourages them from comprehending for themselves
the dimensions of their accomplishment.
Instead of belief in their own worth, their judgment,
they wait for the descent of my pen
to rank them, to ostentatiously present them
with what they already possess.
My pen demands
that each person subject to it
agree that all value lies in the red ink its barrel holds.
Until the nib moves across paper, pronounces its decision,

every achievement, as every failure,
must be perceived as formless, unfathomable,
without moral or social force.
Since the same tool in my hand
provides information, correction, inquiries and
evaluation
—besides extracting obedience—
no wonder the women and men the device affects
become confused about its proper function.

This arrangement
debases my wish to share my knowledge with others,
to test what I show them against their perception
so that we both may better appreciate the world.
My fingers, torn from stringing
a treacherous and hurtful wire,
my hands callused by too many hours
clutching the lash's grip,
award tokens of success, of comfort
that are like blankets infected with disease
whose contagion I cannot escape myself.

Everything I teach
must be weighed against this gift.

THE MUSEUM

Most exhibits here
have been removed
The halls and galleries
display mainly the skill
of their construction
—an intricate carving in stone
at the base of an arch
wood filigree atop a room's wainscoting
ornate metal railings
of staircases and balconies

I bring my classes
to show them the treasures that remain
—portfolios of drawings
ancient bound books and
maps, embroideries
At each visit, less are present
A favorite sculpture
I discover wrapped and tied for shipment
Or I assemble the students
in front of a large rectangle on a wall
that marks where a painting for a hundred years
kept the wall's colour fresh beneath itself
I talk about this absent art
—its technique, the dazzling
contrast of forms
The students become restless as I speak
despite my enthusiasm for the masterpiece
they cannot see

Parts of the museum
are now used as a warehouse
When I wander its corridors
I have encountered young professors
dollying in crates of film
or sealed boxes labeled *Fragile*
and stacking them in empty corners
The piles have vanished
when I next return to the building

My only solace among these losses is
that upkeep of the structure
has been reduced also
Scuffed rugs deteriorate
moldings sag
a hole in the plaster is not filled
Before long, I am certain
somebody will shatter windows
with the damage unattended
One afternoon, snow
will float through broken skylights
and whiten a gallery floor
In spring
weeds will rise through tile
into spaces consecrated to
the human story, offering
another vision
of what we meant to be

USELESS

"All art is quite useless."
—Oscar Wilde

"She points out an old woman,
her chin against her chest, and
identifies her as the former pres-
ident of a distinguished college
for women . . . . I remember her
as a lively, white-haired New
Englander—authoritative, out-
spoken, brisk. She stares at me
with glassy eyes."
—James Atlas

What is not useless? A man frames houses
all his working life, sweat
soaking the front of his T-shirt,
returning to his truck for an old sweater
when the sun drops under the ridge in late afternoon.
Fifty years after he retires
half the dwellings he helped construct
are torn down, and in a hundred years
every nail he hammered or fired into wood
has disappeared.

The winter I built trucks
twenty years ago—or at least contributed my part
to their fabrication—eight a day for eight months:
more than a thousand highway tractors
all junkers by this time
or crushed.

Who are
productive citizens? The crack addict attempting a B & E
who through his efforts erects
the towering edifice of the insurance corporation,
the lock factory, school for tracking dogs,
the latest grad class of lawyers? Or
a vice-president devising a form

to solicit employee feedback on the company's
suggestion for an annual picnic?

Where are the practical men
of Calvinism: the Lords of industry,
their coal mines and textile barns?
What do the great business deals
of the Renaissance amount to?
For what purpose are the skills of the wainwright,
known in several villages,
of the highly-regarded arrow featherer?
Of the acolyte learning the proper rituals
for the worship of Baal, and how to express
God's consolations to the troubled?
The master of Pharaonic art, much in demand
for the tombs of the wealthy
since the King's pyramid was sealed?

Indeed, what is more futile than breathing?
Why should my dentist bother to repair
teeth destined soon for the worms or the fire?
And that larger blaze, our star
that shortly will have burned to no purpose,
absorbing this planet as it flares
into oblivion.
With the absence of the Earth
goes every useless venture,
the ancient activities frozen in ash,
each beautiful hillside with the view of the river,
every object worked or thought by our species.
If humans are still present then,
perhaps transported across the void,
what could a split-rail fence mean to a person
born a millennium after the Earth vanishes?

How useful were any of the accomplishments
of sentient life on another planet in a galaxy
that has already flourished and evaporated?

Yet around my house, hundreds of unavailing trees
put out a million leaves

—not one of which is necessary or important
and in any case will be a brown flake
six weeks from today. I hear a current of air
tremble through these green futilities
and I draw a wind rich with music
deep into my lungs
to permit pointless atoms of oxygen
to be assimilated into blood
that grants me a momentary respite from nothingness
so I can exhale a slide rule
or a song.

BODY MAP

There will always have been
a place named Canada.

Whether a hillside is left
without huge cutblocks where trees once grew

or the administrative areas fracture,
assign themselves other designations

and then split again.
Or if woman by man by child

fresh groups of immigrants
arrive from the South or East.

No matter what happens
to the place called my country,

we, like the tribes before Contact,
existed here.

> My counsellor said, "Tom, stand up"
> and I thought, *What now.*
> He beckoned me through a doorway
> into a room where large sheets of paper
> were taped together on the rug.
> "Lie down on your back," he said
> and when I did
> he traced with a crayon the outline
> of my head, outstretched arms and fingers,
> trunk, legs, feet. I scrambled upright
> while he wound the paper into a huge scroll
> and presented it to me.
> "Make a map," he said.
> "Note the pleasures, agonies,
> and other significant feelings and events
> you associate with each part of your physical self."
> He grinned. "Don't forget any organs."

At home I began to decipher
the occurrences already written in my body.
Why do I prefer my hair long?
How is it tension collects at
the calves of my legs?
Why when I consider my genitals
do I think first of shame?

Finally I stepped back
from my crouch beside the paper,
pen in hand, and saw my being
completely overlaid with words.
Above these phrases and sentences hovered
memories, senses, facts.
After fifty years, I marvelled,
this is who I am. A strange acceptance
suffused me.

We walk and sleep
where others did.

And whichever voices
utter sounds,

we know that for a hundred years
or two hundred—the story is not finished—

this space for a time was called
Canada. The chill wet autumn air,

the August 1918 Vancouver general strike,
an aspen bluff on the prairie

starting to leaf, the Persons case,
the machines removing the rails and then ties

along this stretch of roadbed
one June day, each uncle or student,

landlady or salesclerk
endure in the shape

they help construct,
the form

they influence or determine.
Our shoulders, neck, stomach,

imprinted with laundry and Morgan horses,
wine and nailguns, central processing units,

in turn imprint the land
indelibly—

whatever the mark
says or means.

WAR ON A ROUND PLANET

In the aircraft over a foreign country
a young man from Weyburn, Saskatchewan
throws a toggle switch

and a metal cylinder detaches from the wing
and falls
By this act

the man in the plane
authorizes the destruction of most of a block
of downtown Weyburn—a movie theatre, a bank

a small grocery store with a photography studio
above, a vacant building for lease
—plus several homes in the adjacent street

Fourteen people die
immediately, including six children, and
a woman and a man die later of wounds

despite being evacuated to hospital in Regina
A young woman is blinded
and two men lose a leg and arm respectively

Of the thirty-four other wounded
twelve are off work for more than six weeks
and one man never returns to his former

occupation—farming
No children are orphaned but
several families are reorganized

due to sadness
Eight people suffer some permanent hearing loss
or significant reduction in the use of one or more limbs

and a woman begins a series of outpatient treatments
for mental dysfunction, eventually resulting
in permanent institutionalization

On the ground below the aircraft
a soldier's rifle recoils into his shoulder
At once two shadows depart from the barrel

The echo of the shot races backwards along the sights
around the young man's body
and continues in a straight-line trajectory

over the horizon behind him
Simultaneously, the bullet
spirals forward

in the direction the weapon points
Influenced by a force
more fundamental than gravity

the projectile maintains a constant elevation
as it traverses woodlands and grassy meadows
oceans and orchards

rises over mountain ridges
and descends again above
vineyards or rice paddies

terraced along valley walls
At a speed incalculably swifter than light
the bullet approaches and passes its echo

proceeding in the reverse direction
and homes in on the soldier who released it
who still kneels in the position

from which he fired
"Incoming!" is the last sound
the young man comprehends

CASUALTIES

A petunia
that sways in the garden
cannot hear
rustling leaves of the mountain ash

And a columbine
cannot see its bright yellow petals
or its pinks, nor the purple tubes
of the foxglove
the drooping white of the peonies

Also deaf and blind, geraniums
nevertheless
nod with pleasure
in the breeze, feel the
sudden impatient push
of the bee
into their blossoms
enjoy sun's heat
on stems and leaves
their root-threads extended
in cool wet soil

Marigolds, too, know the sweetness
of pulling water
into themselves
the thick, welcome taste
as grains of nutrient
rise along their stalks
They hate the dust
that filled vein after vein
with a desiccating powder
one dry month

But like the lobelia
they can say nothing

Neither can fuchsias
smell the broom's heavy scent

each evening

like survivors of a tragedy
who sit maimed and bandaged
on a hospital lawn

unaware
of their own beauty

IT WAS MY COUNTRY

> *Era mi patria y estaba desnuda.*
> —Pablo Neruda, "Cordilleras", VI

It was my country
and it was naked

Richard hoists a new window into position
to replace one a grouse shattered

I worked for years in the plant at Lavington
Then the wife and I decided to move out here

I found work installing—mostly windshields, some construction
Glass has been very good to me

Two men stand on the front porch
of Andrea's home in the winter dusk

One pushes the bell
When she opens her door, they hand her an envelope

We no longer require your services as a secretary
Inside you'll find a cheque in lieu of notice

Please give us the office keys
The collection jar is left on the counter

of the country grocery and the village shoe repair
A hand-lettered sign speaks of the couple whose home

was undermined and collapsed due to the unusual runoff in March
And the hour upon hour each day

television needs to, has to be
watched: entire families peer in

like a diver outside the hull of a sunken vessel
who stares through a porthole at a wavering, transformed world

— neck and shoulders tensed, as though to look away
were to miss riches, to forego a revelation

concerning human joy, the chance to be inducted into
mysteries

A man clambers down toward the overturned car
while smoke continues to hover

from the roof's thunderous descent of
the embankment's stones

A woman's hands patiently tend the dying
—the pressure of her fingertips

on ancient skin, reassuring
You are still touched, still valued

by the living
The boardroom decision confirms

another increase in fees
An outline of a statement is routed to

the publicity manager for enhancement
We must remain competitive

We have to appear attractive to investors
And the couple unable to sell their house

now that the market for coal has shrunk
the pulp mill has been declared

uneconomical
Their child wanders through emptying rooms

grasping his toy elephant; his mother
presses clothing into cardboard boxes

that originally contained detergent, vegetables

On the summits that rise

behind the ridge that shadows this townsite
snow burns with the glare of a sunset

occurring far to the west
Under the huge mountains

the air over the highway thickens with
inflowing currents

of darkness:
maritime, uterine

The Clown

THE DEATH OF THE CLOWN

i   a collapsed star

          she radiated gravity

wanting to pull to her
all she lacked:

light
a tattered umbrella

        huge shoes
        time

 a flower to squirt water
coloured discs to juggle

money

ii   she thought her audience was faithless
and it was

turning away
from her beckoning arms

        that demanded
        total attention

no crowd could sustain
                 for long

        she screeched at them
        at their backs
        she honked her horn

the people left

iii   in death, she heard the applause

of silence

her nose dulled
to crimson

then
black

THE BURIAL OF THE CLOWN

There was no funeral.
At the cemetery
not a word was said: mime
with real objects—the coffin
carried from the hearse
over the lawn to graveside
with no noise but indrawn breath.
The pallbearers
were from the Clown Society
but in ordinary clothes,
their sombre faces
free of makeup.

Yet after the casket was lowered
from the chrome frame around the
hole in the earth
and everyone started to leave
except the man with the backhoe

the box bobbed up again.

A member of the burial party
tugged the jacket of the person nearest her
and gestured. This person, too,
alerted others, until all
had reassembled around the coffin
rocking slightly at the surface
over empty air.

A flustered cemetery official
reattached the straps around the casket
and pushed on it.
Once more the wooden box descended
into the ground.
But as soon as the straps were released
the coffin slowly rose
as though the vacant grave

was filling with water
—a ship lifted in a lock.

The third time
the coffin was lowered
the official and two of the clowns
rode it down.
They gathered at one end
while the backhoe
carefully dropped a load of earth
clattering on the lid
and then a second.
The people in the hole
moved to stand awkwardly on the fallen soil

while the backhoe released two more bucketfuls
at the other end.
Then arms reached for the living
and helped them out
as more soil descended.
The casket quivered
        straining against the weight
heaped on it
                forcing down
                        hiding it
away.

When the grave was filled
the ground swelled a little
and the backhoe rolled across the rise
tamping it firm,
level.

No one brought flowers.

THE MONUMENT TO THE CLOWN

GARISH, people said
of the grave marker

    erected in accordance
    with her request

    scribbled in her diaries
    her nieces found

A conical hat
of concrete
five feet high

    angled jauntily
    topped with a large quartz ball

        the whole painted yellow
        with red stripes

        and wired
        —a small endowment
        meeting the electrical bills

            so neon tubing
            in blue

            crackles in a spiral up the stone
            pulsing on and off at random

            and a tapeloop

            emits nonsense syllables
            amid clacks, beeps, water flushing
            kazoos, car-alarm sirens

WE BURIED MY SON SO HE COULD REST IN PEACE
one letter to the editor complained
WHO GAVE PERMISSION

FOR SUCH A DEVICE
TO DISTURB THE SACRED SLEEP OF THE DEAD
Another letter told how the writer
broke into tears when she visited her parents' plot
at Christmas, after travelling two thousand
kilometers, and found
THIS ABOMINATION
WHY SHOULD ANYONE BE ALLOWED
TO MAKE NOISE IN THIS SETTING
LET ALONE DISTRACT MOURNERS
BY FLASHING LIGHTS
Somebody else in print
likened the monument
to the time the cemetery was overrun
with the burrows of ground squirrels
that eventually had to be poisoned
OUR FAMILY CANNOT MOVE OUR DEAD
WITHOUT GREAT EXPENSE
BUT WE WILL IF THIS PROBLEM
IS NOT DEALT WITH

    For those who approach
    the chattering, blinking
    abandoned stone

    the inscription reads
    O Citizen
    Part Of You
    Is Buried Here

THE RESURRECTION OF THE CLOWN

Once she died
she stopped changing
and became so clear

    she could reemerge
    —her bright brittle spunkiness
    her off-key songs

    her delight in balloons
    her dogged
    practicing

        of tap dance
how her body closes in
when she makes love

    her limbs and thighs
    and face
    concentrating

    on joy
These aspects of her
and more

week after week
appeared to
members of the Clown Society

who whispered
about the phenomenon
And former members of her audience

noticed an event
a motion
their memory pulled and twisted

until they could name
where they encountered

her

    In this manner
    she was reassembled
    in other existences

    part
        by part

    until she was reborn
    with her own mind

    altered by the lessons
    death teaches

    to the living

THE CHILDHOOD OF THE CLOWN

alcohol
slapped her
punched a rock
into her stomach: six years old, her parents
gone somewhere
she was found one morning
by an aunt
and taken
her eyes scorched by fear
to be given cold milk
at the tables of an icy
grandmother
uncle

     she lived nowhere
drifting through a family's frowns
with her suitcase:
clothes, a photo of her father
two stones from a week at a beach once
a tiny unicorn

         they said *stupid*
retarded and when she brought home
school praise
they said *who do you think you are*
Miss Bigshot

       she read
any book, and one time
The Lives of the Great Clowns
and again
The Lives of the Great Clowns

THE DREAMS OF THE CLOWN

She wanted white light
showered over everyone

even the evil, the hurtful
revealed as seraphim

but with their nasty-suits on
She desired for herself

a husband
in awe of and love with

how she danced, told
stories in the dark

their babies
She dreamed children

so perfect she blended
their baby food

canned berries
sewed jumpers

in a pink light
She wanted

auditoriums of friends
laughing the palms of their hands

thunderously together
as she bowed from the stage

her-
    self

THE REVENGE OF THE CLOWN

to shape how people laugh at you
mocks
the jeers, their judgments

the grotesque face
the scarlet hair, droopy
clothes
mock the body

her bag lady
spat rage
at a sick universe
—the crowd whistled and shouted
cheered

frightened of her
a little

but loving her
words

the wig itched
she rubbed her finger at the spot
repeatedly

some malevolence
took fire
—cancer of the scalp
the operations
shaved layer after layer
closer to bone, brain

at the hospital
the body that was
clown
and the body
of air and rain
lifted walnuts in turn
to find
the black seed

From a Dark Shore

IN A HOUSE OF WOMEN

in a house of
women, i walk
carefully, watch
my feet on the
rugs, my hands
on the chairs

i avoid these women
when i can, as
in the woods
i avoid bears
or trees

in this house
are Crow-woman
and Turtle-woman, Porcupine
woman and Hummingbird-woman

i recognize their names

but whatever they are, they are not
what i know

just as they
do not know what
they imagine they do

what a man is
for, for example

i hear the women tell each other
they wanted rescue
but the man put them
in a home, to which
he brought back
sperm and money

neither was enough, and
the man also insisted

strict accounts be kept
of each, and the unused portions
returned to him

while he
mostly stayed
in another place

i hear the women say
they and their children
are marooned
when the man did not get
what he wanted
he disappeared, while the woman
who did not earn what she
desired
remains

to responsibly, doggedly
serve
the old
error

in a house of women
a howl
leaps from fingers
settling wildflowers in a blue vase

packages left on counters
hide cosmetics
or poison

outside
the first drops of rain
tap the leaves in the aspen grove
shushing them
for the entrance of
the storm that follows, a frantic downpour

A SAD DAY

A loud *thump*
somewhere in the house
I go look: the grouse
I've heard drumming
at the fenceline under the cedars
is dead on my porch,
neck snapped

       The drumbeat
was like the motor of
a lawn mower or compressor
reluctant to start: pistons
that fire in slow sequence
until the pace increases
followed by, instead of the steady roar
of engine,
silence

      And her voice on the phone earlier
      in tears and rage
      You should be glad somebody cared enough about you
      to be this upset
      and
      I obviously wasn't as big an event in your life
      as you were in mine

      I remember days here
      in fogs of such pain
      when a name and voice
      reverberated through the quiet
      while my mind continually discarded plans
      to mend a shattered bond,
      heal a need

An hour after the grouse's death
I approach the kitchen for coffee
and hear a scuffling
A huge raven
is eating the corpse:

its beak stabs
and rips what is left of the body in half
The black bird hops twice
and flaps airborne toward the trees
with most of the dead thing
between its jaws

Where is that raven, time,
to consume her agony
—to hack at it, chop it
in bits, wolf some down
and carry off the rest

—bird that ate my heart

HARBINGER

Scratches and taps
at a west window

A robin on the ledge outside
eyes me

Then hurls itself at glass
before resettling

to probe the sill with its beak
and then flutters aloft

wings and claws striking the pane
This continues until dark

At first light, I am awakened
by the bird at a different window

For hours, I hear the robin test
opening after opening into my home

What spirit possesses the bird
that it is so determined to come to me?

Who have I wronged this badly?
Who has flown from a dark shore

with a message?
If I allow the bird into my house

what form
will it take? What act

will it accomplish?
What do I refuse

by letting my house
keep me safe from its entry?

WHEN WE PARTED

I was brought
to an offshore island
—one of those rocks that lift abruptly from breakers
to an impossible height, a mesa
in the desert of the sea.
On top, sparse soil
allows the growth of a few cedar and pine
and clusters of grass that bend with the flood and ebb
of ocean light.

And I saw from my perch
a fjord hillside with a settlement
along the water.
From the ridgeline above,
a flow of blocky, jumbled ice
descended, a glacier
that ended just higher than
the village's row or two of homes
and larger structures, dock
and pilings.

I observed a glitter of silver
threading between the sharp angles
and squares of the town:
a meltwater creek
that increased
second by second.
The runnel widened
until the banks on which houses stood
threatened to crumble.
A section of the glacier's lower edge
collapsed,
soundlessly at this remove.
The river eroding the village
surged faster, larger.

I knew I must alert
someone who could help.
I strode to the island's edge

and panicked.
I was far over
the miniature whitecaps on the sea.
I could no longer recollect
how I had been transported here:
by hanglider? Other wings?
I could not jump
from this elevation into the waves.
Nor could I clamber down
the sheer rock walls.
Even if I did
I had no boat.

The view oceanward was
magnificent: tiny combers rolling
to distant white clouds. Salt wind
ruffled my hair.
But I was sick
at the prospect of the drop
into space
on every side, as across the inlet
a glacier
and human order
washed away.

THE ROAD'S SIDE

> "Wayman's closest relationships seem to be with highways rather than women."
>
> —John Harris

Early one evening, Wayman heads out for a drive.
The highway appears pleased to see him,
offering a beautiful curving ascent
like a smooth happy melody
followed by a glide back down like an osprey or raven.
Then the highway seems
to have something on her mind.
Wayman powers through a bend
to encounter warning signs about a flagperson
and a minute later reaches the back of
a lineup of stopped vehicles.
Wayman climbs down from his truck to stretch.
"We need to talk," the highway
informs him. "Ok-ay," Wayman agrees cautiously.
"You know I'm delighted to
spend time with you again," the highway says.
"As a friend, you're wonderful: when you're with me
you give 100 per cent appreciation.
But suddenly you're not available; you're off
doing something else."
"I've been busy,"
Wayman protests: "There's been extra duties at work
and my garden to tend."
"I'm aware these activities are part . . . ,"
the highway states patiently, raising a hand
to deflect Wayman's familiar objection,
"of who you are. But I'm not sure
this situation is what I need.
Do you expect me to simply wait
until you decide to visit?"
"What you want," Wayman proclaims irritably,
"is for me to give up my writing,
my job and my house, and just ride around with you?"
"I didn't say that," the highway responds.

"That's what I hear," Wayman sulks.
"If I'm going to be close to someone
I want him with me," the highway replies.
"I need somebody able to commit.
I value the times I share with you
yet too often you choose to be elsewhere."
"I get the same comment
from women," Wayman protests. "Except they complain
about my being with you."
"They've got a point,"
the highway declares: "My counsellor tells me
a person behaves much the same
in every aspect of their lives. How you treat women
isn't likely to be any different than how you treat me."
From up the line
floats the crescendo of engines starting
and one by one pairs of rear lights
glow redly through the dusk.
"We'll have to finish this discussion
later," Wayman says with relief,
opening the truck door.
"There may not be another opportunity,"
the highway announces.
"I don't believe I can go on like this."
"Let's agree to talk soon,"
Wayman proposes desperately,
noting the van only a few cars ahead
has begun to move.
"I really care for you," Wayman asserts,
"and I don't want to lose the connection between us.
I have to motor over to Kelowna on Monday.
We can talk then."
"Right: once more you'll see me when it's convenient
for you, and are unavailable when it's not,"
the highway observes.
Wayman twitches anxiously from one foot to another
as the car in front of him grinds into gear.
"But I guess I have no choice," the highway sighs:
"We'll talk Monday."
"Okay, Monday," Wayman mutters,
springing into the driver's seat

like a kid let out of school.
At the first crossroad he pulls onto the shoulder,
waits until the lineup behind him passes
and then swings the truck around
steering for home.

ANTHEM: UNDER THE HORNED MOON

Often the crescent moon
sails stiffly vertical

Other times it floats
almost on its back

This night
I am driving I-84 west down the Gorges

into the open arms
of a horizontal horn of light

During my years
beneath the moon's phases

I, anxious and exhilarated,
have steadily felt the road

coming toward me like a spoon
toward a baby

the asphalt pouring under the vehicle's
hood, front bumper

The highway's distances
feed me

As I cover ground,
I am simultaneously racing closer

and away
The motion perfect

perfectly lonely

like this moon

A SELF

On an avenue lined with people
she tries to run a marathon
limping—a knee
and lower leg
are badly skinned, an elbow and
forearm
bleed; her face
is also scraped raw
from falls

To her left, men and women at the curb
politely applaud
and urge her forward *You can*
make it
Keep going; we're proud of you
Brave girl

But along the right, a clump of spectators
jeer and hoot
shout harsh jokes
Hey, speedy, why not learn to walk
before you run
Two bucks says she don't last the block
No way this loser will finish

As the runner stumbles
passing the raucous group
her head turns in their direction
Her mouth sags open
at their insults: that they, anyone
would mock her pain, her
effort
She wants to cry something out
toward them, words to cut
Sensing her anger
the women and men increase their catcalls
Nice roadrash, babe
Who does she think she is
cluttering up the street

with this pitiful performance
Their clamor drowns
the encouragement
from the other curb; tears
stutter down her face
The loudest words
lash her
scald her inner skin
as her ears admit
every sound except praise
except love

"THE EMOTIONS ARE NOT SKILLED WORKERS"

—Ern Malley

The small bird of grief
of love
flits through the dark spaces
between a tree's branches, its leaves
—like an electron
that passes amid the tangled ropes and cords
of the ganglia
in the bush of the brain

Where the tiny creature alights
the twig shudders under its minuscule weight
Electrical conduits short out
and blacken
or part: the tree droops
as though a bear
had blundered up into its structure
ripping and breaking
or an osprey had descended
so the crown of the tree bows to
this temporarily greater
majesty

We need a Marx of the emotions
     We need apprenticeship programs
technical qualification certificates
that must be renewed every three years

The delicate craft required
to shape and machine, to calibrate and tune

is left to driving snow
to the impotent rage of the worms
microorganisms of rot and zygote

thunderstorms of the past

a small brown wren
that decides my fate

IN THE BIRTH CANAL

I once believed
calm achievement
is standard: that toasters
and shopping excursions
normally function without flaw,
that I can expect my interactions with people
to be effective and happy, that what I reach for
is available, unaltered, if at last
my fingers touch it. Setbacks,
denials, collapses
irritated, were wrong
because they were
unnatural. And if my existence
was jangled by
broken fan belts,
defective electrical implements, a serious misunderstanding
about when I promised to phone
then not only were these events a
distortion
of reality
but I was convinced my life eventually would burst out
to a place where such impediments
never disturb the equanimity of an afternoon.

But I became weary of
continual surprises,
dilemmas, failures. When I tallied
ordinary occurrences
and compared them to the results I anticipated
I saw another error.
Now I conclude
nothing is settled or complete.
We are living
in the birth canal.
We may arrive
at a bend of it, a nook in space or time,
and decide we like this—we hang some pictures,
arrange our furniture.
But the floor and walls, even after we unroll

the rug, and apply fresh paint,
suddenly heave and buckle,
and despite our frantic efforts
to keep the lamp from sliding off the coffee table,
to stop the dishwasher from toppling,
to restore the books hurled from their shelf,
we are swept
with our pile of belongings
around a corner.
At first glance the new location
appears familiar, and our impulse is
to sort through our jumble of possessions
and try to recreate the haven we were just expelled from.
But when we examine our surroundings with care
we learn this is unknown territory.

The motion is relentless,
irrevocable.
No matter how far apart the largest contractions,
tremors of change
ripple constantly through our lives.
I know, also,
we will never be thrust into, or otherwise achieve,
any tranquil, static spot.
Just as there is no outside to the curved universe
nothing waits beyond the zig-zag tunnel we inhabit.
The skills I need, then,
are to imagine a better existence here
—to respond less rigidly
to sudden differences, to not feel
claustrophobic, or driven by the need
to have everything controlled
or to control everything;
I want to enjoy or at least be at ease with
the shifting scenery,
the glitches and defeats as well as
the smooth steady run.

In a cosmos with no end but
a start,
a life with the same:

eternal

beginning

THE DARK ONES

The Dark Ones, beings of light
attempt to squeeze through
the fissures between the other side
and a mind even as mediocre
as mine—*whoever*
they say *is*
attentive

        The Dark Ones
bearers of light
console themselves that a root
pushes through earth
and dampness, even stones
to thrive

        what must be sung
they state *throbs like a drum*
a bell
a bead of water on
cedar bark   on antler bone

The Dark Ones are a cave-mouth
that gapes, yawning
in which lightning snakes down
from palate to tongue
The Dark Ones want to come forth
like Lazarus, saved
to save us

        yet they doubt
I am worthy

   Is the soil
worthy? Is gravel?
"The tendril selects
but does not judge,"
I tell the Dark Ones
baby talk they scoff
"I am that baby,"

I insist

      They fall silent
wishing to be clear of me
and in the world, beings of light

     But they must
be carried here
such unworthy beasts
My life   My life

WHERE MOUNTAIN WATER

Where mountain water
rolls stone down from the screes
I knelt
in an alder wood
on an island in that torrent

Around me lay the hammer and crowbar
I had used to break
concrete poured a quarter-century ago
when I had sealed away
my heart

Now through the crumbled cement
I glimpsed pale blue
Carefully I chiselled at rubble
A rich, sour, earthy odor
as of hay
rose from the shrivelled sack
when I eased it
into open air

I held my heart
bloodless, its ghastly bluish tinge
streaked with dirt
and white dust
Its sides felt like
thin pliable cardboard
in my fingers

and I grieved

for all the heart
might have taught me
for what the heart I did not know
could have spoken to women and men
—table-words, bed-words, desk-words
words at the microphone
and by myself in the street
I grieved for the loneliness

of the gap where my heart was absent
and how I have given that lack
to every person
close to me
I grieved kitchens
without butter, a porch
without geraniums, rugs without
candles, roads
with pre-recorded songs

I awoke
and saw on the mountainside behind me
a landscape churned empty by machines
just a few snags standing
a single cottonwood at the rim of a draw
skid trails
stacks of branches
and stumps, roots
heaped
to be burned
The chainsaw, the wheel
of the skidder
were in my hands
—two palms that grasped
what long before had been
my heart

I turned
from my pack and tools
and walked toward the creek
I guessed tears
could not irrigate, rejuvenate
But I planned to wedge the exiled organ
among rocks
to learn if the flowing meltwater
would restore it

I am not sure
if I can ever again
merge with my heart
It seems to me only by

prying myself ajar
with horrible pain
can the blood's universe be inserted
into my body once more
Yet if the heart is flooded, whole
perhaps out on the world-ridge
I will encounter someone to advise me
how I might mend
And if not, at least for joy
and penance
I could walk the rest of my life
carrying a full heart

SOPHIA

As I followed a track
up the valley
the wind on either side

ruffled the crowns of the tall grasses
then pushed the stems nearly flat
and released them

so they shivered with excitement
And on the path
a woman stood whose hair

flowed across her face
like water swirling over stones
a young woman, beautiful

in a simple gown
of richly textured cloth
When I approached

her fingers cleared the wind's work
from her hazel eyes
She raised a hand

to stop me
and said
Does thirst

compel you to carry
that dripping leather bag
in front of you?

Her voice was pleasant
so I began to recite my story:
how I once had entombed my heart

thinking to keep it safe
And how after decades
its absence in my chest

had festered
until the agony
had driven me almost mad

I had managed to disinter
what was left of the organ
yet knew no means

to replace it again in my body
I had soaked my heart
nine days and nights

in mountain water
and now travelled to locate
someone to cure me

if such an act were possible
When I ended my tale
she asked

if she might hold
the heart
I refused, blurting

"This is mine"
Then she laughed, and said
I know how

to return your heart
to you
I was suspicious

and moved to walk on
but she blocked my path
Her eyes were regretful

yet determined
while the wind hissed
Fool! She can help you

become whole
I clutched my burden more tightly
and stepped back from her

as she spoke
You possess your Grail
Thus your quest must be

to relinquish it
The moment
you transfer your heart unreservedly

to another, it will be intact
within you
I felt the weight I hefted

double
and inquired
"Are you the one to receive

my heart?"
She shook her head
When I asked

you denied me
But now that you comprehend
the extent of the task

your road will be lighter
and shorter
She fled by me

down the slope
leaving my heart and I
to the mercy of the wind

the wisdom
of the grass

LA BELLE DAME SANS COEUR

A woman hunkered beside the trail
Bent over, her head propped in her hands,
Her long black skirt, black cloak
A pyramid of grief.

I went to move past.
But she lifted a beautiful face
Damp with tears
To stare toward me. Then she uttered

My name: a question.
I squatted next to her
And realized we had known each other
Years before.

I greeted her; we talked until dusk.
At her suggestion
I set up my tent across the path
From her cabin. We spoke further the next day

And the day following,
Ate meals together.
For a month afterward I remained with her
Helping her as I could

With the chores of her homestead.
Finally, I took my heart
And offered it to her:
It was a Wednesday, mid-afternoon.

But she shrank back, calling out
Her own heart was missing
And that until hers was found
She could accept no other

Which was why she mourned.
She seemed frantic, panicked
At what I held.
I wrapped it away once more.

We watched the dark thicken
Around us, in silence.
We could not see each other.
I packed at first light

And left. When I had travelled
Some minutes I glanced back.
She crouched beside the trail
Face hidden by her hands.

The Bald Man

THE BALD MAN

Some women think constantly
of the bald-headed man

There are stories, rhymes
rituals

And in ordinary hours
the women invite him inside

some shyly, some boldly
to look around

like a contractor
to renovate the kitchen

to replace the wallpaper
or like a mechanic

to solve a problem with the engine
The bald man

sings while he works
Sometimes the melody is

unbearably sweet
as ice cream

sometimes the song is gritty and harsh
—siding scorched by fire

or burnt sugar
If the bald-headed man

likes a woman
(and he likes most women)

he leaves a gift—
usually perfume, seawater

a puddle of floor wax
The gift can be a threat

—a clump of rotted leaves
black and shiny with decay

or even a leech
with a fatal bite

But left behind often
is a basket of puppies

a colt, a stook of marvellous hay
that over nine months

must be spun into gold

INSERTION

When we paused, making love, I returned
down to her aromatic lower mouth
and kissed again the moist opening

Then, desiring more, I placed my head
between her legs
so the top of my body rested

against her vulva
and pushed
She groaned

but said *Yes*
and inch by inch
I eased into her

headfirst
amid terrible cries
and shrieks

Yet she never said *Stop*
Imagine how much love
was shown

by her willingness to suffer this agony
this distention
and cramps

and still to allow
to welcome
this insertion

As the pressure on my skull
eased, and I could feel my shoulders
following, I saw, amazed,

I was in a translucent
cavern, the walls
a luminous pink-orange

like gladiolus petals
with the sun behind them
Now my arms and hands

were within, I could feel
the walls of this compartment
rubbery, slightly damp

like salmon flesh
or an orange anemone
but hot

The sound here
was the double beat/pulse
of her heart

reverberating
in this enclosure
leaving nothing else in my ears but

a faint syllable or two
from outside, and the occasional
muted hiss or gurgle

from her guts
In order to fit
all of myself in

I had to pull my knees
toward my chest
so my toes cleared the opening

which closed behind them
and there I was
safe from the world

I noticed a bulge
to the left of my cheek
where my face touched the wall

and I shifted slightly
which brought the protuberance close to my mouth
and I observed

the mound was like a breast
complete with nipple
so I encircled the end with my lips

and began to suck
and my mind, up to now
turbulent with the adventure

began to hum
the single note
the sole thought

that is intense sensual pleasure
so that after a minute
I could not have said

if I was awake or asleep
or separate in any way
from pure joy

THE NIPPLE

Teahouse of pleasure
after the arduous climb
up the breast

Whether viewed from afar
or close to hand
the nipple is pure
in form and content
as Mt. Fuji
or clear water
By contrast, the vagina
has its opening masked by a thicket
by random folds and crevices
while its functions are blurred
with excretory duties each day
and monthly chores since puberty
Hence the vagina has moods
—scientific, ribald
socially aware
But nipples
are always serious
As the cloth that covers them
is slipped away
the nipples steadfastly meet your gaze
saying *babies*
and again
babies

In this way nipples are themselves
a sort of eye
that demands a statement of your intent
in baring them
you know what we are here for
why we stare at you
No wonder you want to conceal these lidless organs
under the humid basket of the mouth
But when your lips and tongue
enclose the nipple like a holy wafer
and begin to suck

your flesh feels the firm resolve
at the nipple's core
its single-minded dedication
its adult
purpose

THE BIG O

*A poet is allowed to use the
interjection O just once in a
lifetime.*

—rule for writing

Each time I face the fleshly o-
val, the folded and enfolded entrance
with its hairy cap
I wonder
is this it?
is this the O I am permitted?
The tongue, teeth
my whole mouth
working diligently
delicately
draft after draft after draft
is this sweet flow I suck
the Muses' fount that
rises in the cleft
struck by Pegasus?
When a version works
each breath
I take, release
each tongued syllable
vibrates all Mount Helicon
quake after quake

In another version
the seismic probings
that trigger shock
below ground
cause ripple upon ripple to curl
across the field of her belly
—the tempestuous earth-surf
threatening to swamp
the coracle of the navel

Such moments
bring us closer

every time
to the bel-
    low ringing
the pro-
longed ye-
    ES
and counter to
all laws, the
O the   O the
O

EXCAVATION

She came and subsided
and my middle finger resumed
lightly coasting above
her vulva, then as her breathing altered
the tip descended
deeper into the slippery passage again
The finger's shaft
pressed gently on and around the nub
that had risen on the upper slope

    Yet as my finger pushed
    further within
    the pad touched
    something angular, unfamiliar,
    wooden
    I hooked it
    and eased it out to the light
    It was a miniature chair
    Not like dollhouse furniture
    but a perfect replica of a
    real kitchen chair
    I placed the object to dry
    on the bedside table

Absorbed in her pleasure, she seemed unaffected by
this interruption
The whole incident was as though
one of us shifted position
to free a limb from under somebody's weight
I quickly returned to my caresses
but my trolling finger
snagged
on what felt
cylindrical, or ropy
When I lifted the obstacle clear
it was a tiny, obviously-used vacuum cleaner
—like the chair
an accurate reproduction
only shrunken in scale

With some trepidation
my hand entered her once more
and drew out
a set of dinner plates
The nightstand's surface
rapidly became crowded with
drying household goods
—floorlamp, rug, bookcase,
spice rack, electric lawn mower

This archaeological exploration
by now had altered
the pace of our lovemaking
My growing wonder
at what next would be revealed
had supplanted passion
She must have sensed
this shift, because suddenly her hand
intercepted mine above her thighs
Her eyes opened
and she sat up

      She smiled at me
      wrenched a pillow behind her
      and leaned back, sighing
      That was great
      But am I thirsty
      She bent to take a sip of water
      from a glass on the night table
      and noticed the jumble of miniature objects
      piled as in a moving van
      She turned toward me, astonished
      What are these? she asked
      Why didn't I see them before?
      Are they yours?

GRANDFATHER AND GRANDMOTHER

Genitalia after puberty
are old
even on young bodies
—wrinkled, sagging
spotted by random hairs

Along with canines and molars
the penis and vagina
clearly survive from more primitive times

Genitals conduct themselves
like a grandmother or grandfather
who expects obedience
In our teens and early 20s
they are shrilly insistent
Have you no respect for your elders?
When I ask you to do something for me
I want it done
and I want it done right now
and I don't want any back talk

Yet by our 40s we recognize
our grandparents are not particularly wise
or prudent
We begin, at first haltingly
to assess their demands
Though I love you, we tell them
I'm not going to contribute
to behavior I believe is destructive
I refuse to be a codependent
to your dysfunctions

The grandparents become outraged
muttering *ingratitude*
and *you've changed, changed for the worse*
Yet they have no choice
but to accede to our decisions
only complaining loudly to their opposite numbers
whenever they meet

how self-centred
and heartless
the grandchildren are

THE NEST

"Y la sombra es el nido
cerrado . . . "
            —Miguel Hernandez

Now shadow is
the closed nest
—tangled shadow: fibres
of a coarse mound
or effervescent tendrils

The nest
may be clenched
or darkly willing
—ready to open, trembling
because of events
thousands of kilometres
distant
or near to hand,
cajoled, teased, impressed,
so many kisses,
breathed on, spoken to
in tongues, answering
in the glossolalia
that remains an authentic
language of the nest

And now the nest is
dim water
—mysterious moisture
on the canyon floor,
rivulet or pond
constrained by shale banks,
then a creek
dodging past bullrushes,
coarse grass,
widening toward
swamp maple, flowering broom,

an odor of birdsong

that flickers amid the reeds,
river-bottom of clear sand,
sharp calls of robin,
wren, nuthatch,
attar of wild rose,
the slow lift of heron,
hulking pelt of bear
disappearing between
cottonwoods

But when light
becomes the nest,
a beam of fire,
a glowing orb,
conjoin,
flash
like molten metal
sparkling, or a fire
that has caught on fire,
where flame breaks out
atop other flames

in whose radiance
the faces, bodies
of grandparents,
grandchildren
swirl, ablaze
in a nimbus, glory

Cities, too,
cabinetry manuals, scythes,
jet engines
nestle in that scorching cup

nest of ancestors
nest of world

LIFE WITH DICK

My dick wakes me
in the night
Hey, I have to pee
Get up
"What?" *Up, up*
This is urgent
I look at the clock
—two a.m.
But my dick doesn't care
No more snoozing for you, buddy
until I take a leak
I stumble into the can
go about my business
and collapse between the sheets again
I pull the warm blanket of sleep
over my head
but a nudge in the ribs
stabs me into consciousness
"Huh?" *Now I'm not tired*
my dick announces
and I notice its jaunty appearance
Say, big boy
it whispers amorously
How about, you know, you and I . . .
"Forget it," I snap
"I *need* to sleep
I have a huge pile of work to accomplish tomorrow
whereas you'll spend the day
loafing as usual"
I realize I've insulted it
as soon as I utter the words
It stiffens even more
and turns its back to me
We lie like this: it sulking
and me furious
at its choice to express its emotional demands
in the middle of the goddamn night
"Okay," I finally state
"Maybe on the weekend

we can do something together
This just isn't an appropriate time"
I hear it sniff with contempt
at my conciliatory gesture
Yet a minute later
I can tell its stand is softening
That's a promise? it inquires
"Sure," I pledge
All right, then, it murmurs
Next instant my alarm
is frantically tugging the covers off me
as if the house is on fire
or some other disaster is imminent
I shut down the buzzer
and lie back groggy

Oblivious to the noise
and to my appalling lack of rest
my dick sleeps on like a baby

Billy: A Pastoral

THE VALLEY BY NIGHT

In the hours
when dawn is neither hope
nor memory
I hear
a cough
thick with phlegm as an old man's
gagging and
throat clearing
and know that Billy
has come out to stand on his deck
and smoke, since Joan
won't let him light up indoors

His feverish bark
echoes
at the edge of the sleep
I fall into again
like the semis
hauling through the darkness
across the River
or when coyotes
up Pedro Creek
or closer
start their wail
and the Valley dogs agree and disagree

or the silence I wake to
and hear from the woods above Warner's fields
an owl
and again an owl

BILLY'S PECCADILLOS

Conrad stops me
coming out of the store:
That your lawn mower
in your trunk?
Good.
The community cemetery
grass needs cutting
Can you do it with me?
I would, I reply, except
I'm on my way to take the mower
back to Sears: the deck is cracking.
Look here: both places
where the handle joins.
This is the second time
in a year and a half
this has happened.
But, hey,
how about Billy?
I know he and Joan have
two lawn mowers.
He'd likely be glad
to volunteer.

Can't ask Billy.
The woman who lives next door to
the graveyard
used to go with him.
It didn't end well.
I wouldn't want her
to look out a window
and see Billy that
close.

REVEREND BILLY

How old is Billy? His eyes
bright with the excited laugh
of a teenager pleased by
a new car or
a concert ticket
for a band he loves. Yet his face
hammered into ditches
and scars from the years
chained to drinking
—that time now past.
He has watched his lovers' children
grow to the gate of adulthood
and pause.
They see his forty summers
a road leading two ways:
not quite parent, nor
young. His friends, as well
watch him, measure their progress
and defeats
by his: priest
of Janus, god of
portals,
offering another chance,
the grace of
possibility

BILLY ON INDUSTRIAL PROGRESS

He's down in the big garden
on a cold day
early November
before the snow
having left the autumn rototilling
this late, and Joan's old machine
can't really handle
the frozen topsoil
or maybe the icy temperature
but in any case
the engine dies every few meters
and when it does start again
the machine spurts ahead as the tines
suddenly climb on top
of the hard ground
and race across the surface
snapping Billy's head back
as he's yanked after
until he gets the device
settled in again
and turned to cover the part of the row
it missed

At the moment, though
the rototiller is on its side in the dirt
having stalled out once more
and Billy is looking at it
like he'd kick it
except he knows he would kick it so hard
he'd break his foot
and that would hurt
too
so instead he stands in the field yelling
to inform the crows and jays
nothing has gone right for the human race
since the industrial revolution
and the Luddites were right
wanting to smash all machinery
and there are people in this Valley

he knows, personally
who will tell you the wheel
was invented by a woman
and since the wheel is the basis
for every machine ever invented
it isn't hard to point the finger
at just who is responsible
for things being
the way they are

BILLY AND HOUSING

To some locals, he's
The-Guy-Who-Burned-Down-His-Cabin
Yeah, he says sheepishly
when I ask. *Three years ago*
before I stopped drinking
I was drunk and probably stoned, too:
fell asleep in front of the TV
one of those big old upholstered chairs
cigarette, woke up to smoke
the arm of the chair was in flames

Now here's the goofy part:
I could probably have
picked up the chair and tossed it outside
through a window or even the door
But I panicked
ran into the snow
over to a neighbor's since I didn't have a phone
By the time the fire truck showed up
the shack was too far gone to save

Literally burned to the ground
And I didn't grab so much as my jacket
when I left, with my wallet in it
I'm standing outside, 37 years old
zip to my name

BILLY ON THE VALLEY

People come here
especially in summer
look around
at the mountains
the River
the forests
the Lake
exclaim
It's paradise
A green paradise

I've been here five years
I tell 'em
Green
hell

BILLY AND WOMEN

My technique, *Billy said*
when I have to talk to a beautiful woman
is to imagine her
with the skin off: heart and stomach
esophagus and lungs
liver and intestine
all exposed
with veins and arteries
everyplace
Seeing a woman this way
helps me respond to her as
human, as a person
so I'm less
self-conscious

INTRUSION

Shouts out of the black
of an August night
from the road at the bottom of my drive:
repetitive, angry cadences
of a drunken confrontation:
You asshole
That ain't fucking good enough
Myself and two Saturday visitors
drinking ourselves since dinner began
listen with the glee
of reading somebody else's mail
Okay, now I'm really *mad*
and then the harsh sharp sound
of metal dented
and louder yelp words
from the dark
"They're getting serious"
somebody at the table observes
and one of my visitors sways to her feet
and moves onto the porch to overhear better
Indoors, the tedious rhythm of ascending and descending volume
swells and fades through the open window
Then silence
And a car coming up the drive
"Surely she didn't go down
and bring them up here," I protest
but she did, and I head outside
angry now at having to deal
with the unknown

It's two young men I've never seen before
and one of the arrivals, Paul, wants praise
as the peacemaker between his buddy
Fred here
and Ron after Fred wouldn't stop hitting
Ron after Ron had been punched to the ground
forcing Paul to pull Fred off Ron
and smash Fred against the car
so hard it fucking bent the fender, man

Hey, Fred's my buddy,
But when a man's down, he's down, eh?
You back off Fred has a different opinion
of course
Yet since Ron apparently has gone away on foot
snuffling back blood
I think I fucking broke his nose, man
the event is over but the telling
and retelling
until at last they are reversing their car
although half-way down my drive
get stuck at right angles
the rear fender lodged in the bank
before they are free, spinning gravel, and their lights vanish

Next afternoon, I'm weeding the garden
when a rusty Toyota
rises up the drive
It's the boys again
who say they came to apologize
although it's clear they really want to find
the Angel of the Dark whom they recall appeared suddenly
where they were arguing on the road
"She's not here," I break the news to them
"She and her sister left this morning"
The apology becomes first on the agenda once more
A nearly-empty bottle of rye is fished out
and placed on the hood
and since they're obviously around until the whisky is finished
I relax
although I don't invite them in
and don't go in myself when my phone rings
I learn Paul is a miner
just had his thirtieth birthday
and they were drinking yesterday because
his appointment with a Compensation doctor
got postponed another twelve months
I make lots of money on Compo
$2,000 every two weeks
but I like to work
I don't enjoy this hanging around

I worked in Peru once
four days off in two years
One of those years I paid $40,000
in income tax
Paul was run over by an underground train
I was busted up pretty bad
They said I'd never walk again
Look He leaps up and his airborne heels touch
But they didn't put me together quite right
He pulls at one pantleg
to display a massively scarred leg and knee
Watch this
He grabs his knee and shifts it
several directions a knee can't move
Show him your foot, man
Fred suggests
They didn't sew his fucking foot on straight
and sure enough Paul's left foot bends off at an angle
compared to his right
They say I can't go back to work
until all this is corrected
but they keep rescheduling my appointment
Are you sure you don't want
some of this rye?
Only one doctor in the province
who can do the operation
and he has to see you
before he'll operate
Now I gotta wait another twelve months
Hey, I'm not like these people on welfare
I like to work

He and Fred met at the start of the summer
both newcomers to the Valley
Paul had married a woman from here
I just knew her two months
We were both lonely, I guess
But she left me to live with a former boyfriend
You know what's weird?
She and I never even had a fight
Fred came out from Ontario

to see more of the country
I'm heading back at the end of the month
No fucking jobs here
Listen, there's your phone again
Don't you want to answer it?
His arm, when he lifts the plastic glass
has *Extra Old Stock* tattooed on it:
the brand of beer where a woman's name might go
Yeah, first I'll patch a few of the holes in this shitbox
He kicks the car affectionately
Cops in Ontario get heavy if you have too many gaps
Then I'll be on my way
He smiles his bad-toothed grin
Fuck-all happening
around this place

As they depart
they offer one more choral
set of apologies
plus promises to visit again
I walk east of the house
to watch them disappear
and see Billy leaning against his deck rail, smoking
He climbs down
and ambles toward the fenceline

Friends of yours?
he asks, and when I finish my explanation, adds
I kept phoning over
to see whether you wanted help
I figured the phone would give you an excuse
to escape
I wondered if they thought
it was you called the cops on them last night
Actually, I was the one who phoned
but before the Mounties showed, those bozos had gone
I worried they might have been picked up nearby
and came back because they were choked about it
That's just your guilty conscience, I tell him
He chuckles, then
I think I know the Ron

they were fighting with
He's local; belligerent when drunk
Rowdy Ron, they call him
A big guy, but a pushover in a fight
Almost everybody around here who drinks
has been in a tussle with him one time or another
including me
People eventually realize
there's no glory in having punched out Ron
Now he is mostly left alone
Billy stubs his cigarette
on the bottom of his boot
knits his fingers together
and stretches
Since the excitement is over
I better cut the grass
before Joan gets back
But keep me informed if any other of your friends
are yelling at night
I'll just ignore them
After all, what are neighbors for?
And we both turn away to resume the tasks
of an aging summer

BILLY EMPLOYED

He knew everything
about everybody
for nearly ten kilometers
north and south of the Crossroads Cafe
both sides of the River
I'm a fresh air inspector, Tom
Let's face it
I'm bone lazy
I'm the laziest person I know
Wait—I know one guy
lazier than I am
He did establish projects:
to learn how many consecutive days
he could go swimming, and
to eliminate sword ferns
from the cleared area by the woods
west of the lawn

Then he applied to be
and was hired as
a caregiver for the elderly
—first part-time
but he kept requesting more hours
and the agency liked his work
so he was hardly ever around
I've gone from unemployed
to workaholic
in seven weeks
He didn't have any information
on the guys who looked like bikers
living in a teepee during July and August
in the bush along the Lower Road
Haven't had a free moment
to walk past
or to ask anybody
And there's a full-time position
coming up
they want me to apply for
which he got

and obtained with the proceeds
a new pair of sweatpants
a used pickup truck
and began to talk about
how much he would enjoy
a satellite dish
to watch football

The Call

THE CALL

Rain in gusts all day
that slackened a little at dusk
but the night
dripping. I sat
in my room
in the dormitory at the edge of the woods
by the edge of the sea.
As I finished a page
in the glare of my desk lamp,
as my fingers caught the paper's upper right corner
to turn it
I heard a voice
—urgent, but without sound—
Go outside
I glanced through the window
at the drizzle
lit with walkway lights.
Again the voice suffused me:
You must go outside
The tone was uncompromising.
Go out and
across the road Impatience
vibrated in the words
and a sense I was being drawn
to a purpose: a moment
or presence

        I stood,
uneasy. But I walked downstairs,
through the main doors
and felt the first drops soaking into my shirt
to skin. The voice remained certain:
Across the road
Enter the forest

On the closest shoulder of the highway
I paused.
I peered over at the tangle of underbrush and
evergreens. I saw only

rain.

The voice propelled me forward.
On the other side of the road
I halted that much nearer to the woods,
shivering in the chilled damp of my clothes.
Black sky. Heavy downpour now. Wind in the
cedars' gravely swaying tops.

What would meet me in the dark?
Nothing but branches and roots
and the massive trunks of the trees
showering me
with winter rain:
icy ocean's breath
calling me *fool*

Or a tall man
waiting ahead in a clearing
—one eye socket horribly scarred,
a raven walking the wet ground
at his feet,
a horse nearby
cropping grass in the forest's
deep silence

Or a fire far off
that as I approach
I see is ringed with
cloaked human shapes
seated at the hissing flames
A face—now male, now female—
lifts in my direction
as I struggle in the drenched brush
toward them

I trembled
to guess the unknown I was called to
Because I could not understand in advance
this event
I was afraid

Then the sound was the drops
driven by the gale against the hard
surface of the road
and the leaves.
Behind me, past a lawn, the dormitory
rose through rain like a lighted ship.

I turned
to look at the building's doors, stairs,
my room. I began to
retreat.
Yet the instant I swung away
I knew I had spurned a great summons
or gift,
an enormous
chance.

SKY GRAVITY

I read certain poems
and think how much they are like my dreams

While I am with them, I cannot turn away:
my mother after her death
explaining she has chosen to sleep on a mat on the floor
because she spread cloth on the bed
for a pattern she is sewing
and does not want to disturb it

Yet most dreams
do not mean
enough for me to remember
An intensity is absent
or erased by daylight

                    *   *   *

Where I cannot comprehend writing
or the words' feelings or ideas
are flat for me
or my mind veers off—
a tire losing purchase on ice

I am shown again the mystery
of how the shaped lines of letters
can call out the world
only after we have undergone
a revelation
—the child for a second time laboriously guides
a pencil through the path of his name
—at the edge of the lake, water pours from a ewer
over the hands of the initiate
while other hands hold a basin, a towel
and a strip of linen rich with embroidery

                    *   *   *

through the blackness, the wind

bellows out the side of the tent

a train in the mountain night
releases its long delicious horn

an owl calls six notes
and repeats

        *   *   *

in the distance, a cloud
lets down the rain

as though the mass of the storm
were a sky fire, and the downpour

is smoke from that blaze
climbing toward the earth

POETRY OVERDOSE

Each day on the planet
a million poems are written
Of these, English-speaking North America
accounts for roughly ten per cent:
a hundred thousand poems
In a year, then
more than thirty-six million
appear on this continent
on lined paper, notebook pages
and computer printouts
I have no proof
these numbers are correct
but they sound right to me
And, as any poet knows, if something sounds good
it must be true

Of the thirty-six million poems produced here annually
maybe one day's worth succeed in being published
—in a plum, mass circulation magazine
or in the fifty copies of the first and last issue
of a photocopied venture
intended to save the art form from being marginalized
Perhaps ten thousand of these printed poems
appear again in their authors' books
during the following three years:
whether volumes issued by a nationally-distributed press
or a collection the poet pays for herself or himself
tries to sell at local readings
and eventually gives away
About a thousand of the poems in books
get chosen over the next five years
for anthologies
—thematic, ethnic, geographic
And at the end of ten years
of these thousand anthologized poems
only sixteen
are still being reprinted
although during this interval a few thousand others
have flashed an additional time and died

in a handful of poets' selected poems

From more than thirty-six million
to sixteen
in a decade
is such a rate of attrition
no wonder we never stop
jotting down phrases
jabbing at keyboards

With poems, as with mosquitoes
millions must be born each breeding season
so a pitifully small percentage
can annoy you when you try to sleep
give you satisfaction when you smack them down
draw blood

THE GENIUS

A group of us
crowd up to the table
where the man stretches his palms over the word
he has formed from large wooden letters
that resemble a child's toy

Before our eyes
his hands lift the power
out of the word

His fingers conceal
what he has extracted
Yet a radiance filters through
as though sunlight is leaking between his clasped hands

I am in awe of this skill
—convinced he could use this power
in a vital cause: to transform lives
for the better, defeat enemies
destroy an injustice

But he seems nonplussed
by our continuing to gape at him
now that the word's essence has been obtained
He shrugs once, as if to say
Show's over, ladies and gentlemen
No one moves
He remains with hands tightly together
face embarrassed, staring down at the letters
I imagine what I might do
if I mastered this ability
To him, I think, *this is just a trick
he can accomplish*
People begin to drift off
After we disperse, I wonder
will he return the power back to the word?
He holds his fingers like they imprison
a moth

THE COLOURS OF THE FOREST

I wandered on the bank of a stream
in the sunny afternoon
and discovered where two logs had been placed
to bridge the water

and I crossed

The creek was sluggish, braided
into pools and boggy puddles
between cliffs down which aspen spilled

A hawk
rode July winds over the coulee
Squirrels rehearsed their staccato protest

And I noticed a gate or stile
of poles
blocking a small gully
that descended toward the stream
There was no fence, only the poles I climbed through
and entered under the canopy of poplars
A clearing stretched ahead
wide as a road, yet I could not see stumps
or any other indication
this space was not natural
Underfoot, when I followed the opening
were low grasses and ferns
as though the area had been mowed
Small birds darted among the branches
on either side, settling and rising in groups, like fish
if fish could pipe and whistle
Insects spoke loudly, monotonously
I heard the hawk cry overhead

Hiking that dappled road, I felt
suffused with a joy
tangible as a song
that rang amid the trees, its tones and rhythm and words
fashioning a world

that never before existed
And the absence in this wood
of familiar human myths and presences
was strong enough I sensed
I was led along this route
by another kind of being
or beings
who sang together in pleasure
Yet some dark aspect of me started to complain
about the brevity of the afternoon
how my happiness at
the sunshine bright as clouds
on the upper surface of the leaves
this portion of only one day
must soon end
But the light breathed into pulsing fire
yellow scents and green sounds
And how the light released
all the colours of the forest
argued that for these moments
beauty
      suspended
            time

And while these voices
of discontent and music
raged in my head
I thought they merged into flowing water
until they were drowned by flowing water
and I came upon a brook
scurrying between stones and roots
—a tributary, I guessed, of the languid stream
I had left behind

Where the busy water crossed the road
that was not a road
a pool had been formed or dug
in the shaded earth
When I stepped closer
I saw a wooden ladle, roughly carved
hung by its handle above the basin

I knelt by the pool's edge
—on one knee only, as the Bible cautions
—and reached for the dipper
and brought the icy fluid to my lips
So intensely cold, this nectar
seemed sweet to my tongue and throat
I swallowed and felt this water
flow through my limbs like cooled blood
I knew I was not the first to drink here
nor the last
I rehung the ladle on its branch
I understood this was an honor given me
greater than the day
—to have been brought to this fountain
to have drunk
It could not matter whether I was the best or worst person
to be shown this spring
I drank
and the water filled me
and the sun and moon shone down through the trees